Russell Jones has published six collections of poetry and edited three poetry anthologies. He is the deputy editor of Scotland's only sci-fi magazine and was the UK's first Pet Poet Laureate. Russell also writes books for children, young adults and supposedly-grown-up adults. He has a PhD in Creative Writing from the University of Edinburgh and occasionally blogs at:

www.WriterRussellJones.blogspot.com

cocoon

poems by
Russell Jones

featuring artwork by
Sara Julia Campbell, Caroline Grebbell,
Aimee Lockwood, Edward Ross,
& Mark Toner

Poems from *cocoon* have also appeared in *Aiblins: New Scottish Political Poetry*; *Atrium*; *Buenos Aires Poetry* (translation Spanish); *Carers UK Anthology*; *Causeway/Cabhsair*; *Coast to Coast to Coast*; *Dark Matters*; Edward Ross' *B-sides & Shorts*; *Forty Voices Strong*; *Glasgow Review of Books*; *Gutter*; *Ink, Sweat & Tears;* Lies, Dreaming; Poetry Tree at Oxford Museum of Natural History; *Rialto; Seen/Unseen; Some Cannot Be Taught;* Talbot Rice Gallery; *The Scotsman; Young Poets, Scotland* (translation Greek).

* * *

Published in 2020 by Tapsalteerie
9 Anderson Terrace, Tarland
Aberdeenshire, AB34 4YH
www.tapsalteerie.co.uk

© Russell Jones 2020

Russell Jones has asserted his right under the Copyright, Designs and Patents Act, 1988, to be identified as Author of this Work.

Illustrations are copyright of the respective artists.

ISBN: 978-1-9162148-1-1

Printed and bound by Imprint Digital, Upton Pyne, Devon.

JC
JM
JJ

lie of the land • 9

lyceum • 14

dark horse – **art by Sara Julia Campbell** • 15

by insisting on love we spoil it • 17

versus • 18

skives • 19

the flame • 20

scrump • 21

aqueduct • 22

the pink river dolphins of peru • 23

salt 'n' oats • 24

apples for grandma – **art by Edward Ross** • 25

wash day • 29

you gotta go there to come back • 30

cat out the bag • 32

abigail • 34

kintsugi • 35

kabuto • 36

anatman • 38

anitya • 39

the 200-year-old monk • 40

songbird • 41

pioneer • 42

an official guide to surviving the invasion

  – **art by Caroline Grebbell** • 47

quiz night at the palm gardens hotel

  – **art by Mark Toner** • 50

the alligator get-out clause • 53

the counting house • 54

the good thief • 55

howls • 56

october 29th • 57

the races • 58

hog • 59

biography of a cow • 60

beorn – **art by Aimee Lockwood** • 61

ignition • 65

boatswain • 66

let us be mauled by the ocean • 68

a sleep • 69

up the garden • 70

balloons over bagan • 72

aurora photography • 74

acknowledgements • 76

lie of the land

I

Come out from your cave, lichen
flourished on each wall, cream white
smoke and lips. Come out,
gander at the stars – brittle lights
that end when you sleep.
Hunt for your children, plough deep
with torn nails, paint with blood,
dig meat from your teeth.

Some day the land may recoil,
but now the ivy creeps
with tracks real as death.
Every tree throttles,
every vine is set to snap
at your feet. Stay quiet, listen
to the fire cackle, the pigs
screaming in the night.

II

Reel and fish eyes, a wash
where walrus men plant
their feet and sun
loungers, dream
of waffle cones
and thirty-years-ago
sex. They let time spill
with their guts, let waves
lick at their toes,
look for mermaids,
cast out
without lines or hooks.

III

Up, to the rigorous stone
claws of the steady mountains.
Clouds shrink from their heads,
yet we've marked our boundaries
by their skyline. Look out
to gravestones, fissured rock
walls, to millennia-dead sheep
whose wool still brushes the quarries
in a breeze, like the stories we share.
We continue to bore our children
as our parents did, but force them to listen.

IV

Build a matchbox casket for poor old Tom.
Peter's cast himself from a window sill.
The miller's daughter's turning straw.
Mary's lambs have gone to pasture.

Tonight, light the fire, tease
the scatty mice from their hiding places
with foreign cheese. Sharpen the knife
and put it away, but keep it sharp.

V

The city's dark and distant. Ice
shears from car windows.
You ride by towers of glass,
the streets littered in heads
spiked during the commute.
You travel alone, not stopping
when the lights turn
to amber. Hurry, or the storm
will steal you from the ground.
Beep the horn. It is the only way
to feel the blood in your fists,
to make a sound in a world of noise.

lyceum

Pretty in their summer dresses, tuxedos,
they glide like swans on concrete lakes
    towards the glass foyer, tickets
    flapping in gold webbed feet,
        past the pigeon man
          who pecks the wall
            with his soft beak
              he pecks, he pecks,
                he pecks until
                  the glass is red.

Dark Horse

On summer nights this city's rarely dark.
The sun's an insomniac child, glancing out
from the curtain of clouds.

Soon, it will swim
over hidden corners, tease blossoms from buds,
show us our boundaries, shorelines and caves.

I live for darker days,

drape a scarf over my shoulders

Walk into the empty, early morning, fold into shadows.
My fists and feet harden into hoofs, I brush my hair into a mane, spine cracking into a saddleless back
as my tail grows long, sweeps litter from the paths.

I test the miles a horseman can run,
the cobbles fissuring beneath my track.

Launch my new legs through
the neighbourhoods.

by insisting on love we spoil it
– Jack Gilbert

To sit is enough, so we do: on the too-big sofa,
a coast train, in hookah cafes, minds like smoke
and buttered fingertips. Ask for a shadow and I'll cast it
for you. In the house we bought together, our nursery
is unlikely to be filled. Fine, soon we'll see the green light
of Borealis through the toilet window. Let's tear the sky
down but be assured – unknowing isn't the half of it.
The universe is tiny if we call it out; but each fold
makes another crease we've not yet explored.

versus

Nobody warned me that you'd strike so fast
in the bedroom where we'd played for years.
Doll on doll, car chasing track, spies
among the mountain caves. You take off

your chequered shirt, tie it around your head,
commando-style, a warrior atop the bed,
pillow high and disrobed. Feathers fly,
old games are thrown aside. These hours

of tongues and hips are our initiation trials.
I think to Indiana in his temple of doom:
nerves steady, love-soured, hat tipped,
whip ready, his heart almost ripped

from his ribcage. You lunge as I whistle
his theme tune. Soon, you've beaten me
back, your lips sucking at my neck and all
we know is each other, that the venom must be

taken in to be taken out. Morning is brief.
An alarm rings, we wrap up in the sheets,
check for scars, that our hearts are still
in our chests, hope love never saw us coming.

skives

Young and troubled, together
behind the headstones, we purged
the epitaphs, pulled the flowers
from their ceramic nests, tapped
the sacred ground for worms, whispered,
This won't bring back the dead.

We pocketed the violet pebbles.
Back then, we felt unholy – we hid
from their ceremonies, talked
god, kissed, but never prayed.
The church bells drowned us
out with white weddings, babies
blessed, bodies for our graves.
The congregations marched
like soldier ants, black and busy.

But mostly I remember the old girls
who'd visit on quiet days.
We'd sit in silence, watch them
resist their handkerchiefs.
Sometimes they cried, sometimes they didn't.
We liked their origami lips, trembling
as if they still had something folded away.

the flame

You keep the candle for him, you say, a reminder
that every life is a flame. Though you can't be sure
which night was his conception, you strike a match,
light the wick. We pour hot wax across our palms
to purge the pain, watch it cool and crack.

We think back to when we were kids, how we spent
our evenings playing shop, Scalextric, happy families;
how we dipped our fingertips into pools of wax.
It was our game, our torture. We let our hot shells harden,
peeled them away to make petals. Then, before the blaze
was out, we set them back like boats on still water,
watched them melt and be reclaimed.

Now he's gone, your face is set. You say you want to burn
an eternal flame for him, so he'll never be put out
of mind. I take out my lighter and we wait
for the wax to turn to tears. We dip
our fingertips, blow them gently,
peel away the petals, let them melt again.

scrump

Dad's the only god I'll need. Recall the coos
from wet-perm women, enough to keep
the small town talking for a decade.

Recall the car rides, the offie, blue bags
built for house party booze, ciders
for under-sixteens, the sodden fumbles.

Man, the distance only improves.
Recall the apple: green, pulled apart
at the seeds, know all gods are fanciful.

Study, screw about, make your home
in the orchards. Recall the wildfire, drink
enough to keep your old man talking.

aqueduct

Summer, the aqueduct fermenting in the midland
heat. Walkways rotten or overused; fat maggots
turning in the mouths of fishermen, hooked as bait;
the smell of flesh and sawdust in the sun.

We waited for the long days to pass, to sit
out by the empty fishing spots, two rubble bags
beneath us, two litres of cider from the corner shop.
Those nights were peaceful, private

among dragonflies, bats, white-throated
frogs testing new waters. We smoked, talked
dirt, pulled up grass, our hands skimming
stones across darkened surfaces.

We were silent when the walkers passed,
not wanting to be found. Finished, we staggered
to our bikes, said *Catch you later,* rode shoddily
home down the dim-lit, fish-hooked streets.

the pink river dolphins of peru

She lay on the banks of the Amazon, sang
of capybara: *Oh, my long-tooth love,
great guinea, come to me, come.*
That was all: near-innocence,
wet hair drying.

It grew dark, she tells the town,
months later when she swells
like spring waters. *I was alone.*

So they gather with dead fish
to tempt him. He bites,
chatters, pink as cantuta,
stands accused.
They don't need more evidence
than his serrated, erectile jaw,
his guilt-loaded eyes.

Waters break, the town floods
in to see her birth. Human scream
from bottle nose, waving five-prong
flipper, umbilical or blowhole.

It's common here, the midwife reports.
*A real myth. Please, stay away
from the riversides.*

salt 'n' oats

This could help you live
forever: warm the water
in a milk pan, add your oats,
stir in salt, let it rest.

Take breakfast in the woods:
listen to the birds, find a house
ridden with hair. Test the beds.
Should you be woken, run.

Don't stop – the bears are furious,
honed on your scent, quick.
Let them follow. Set the traps.
Wait until the wood is silent.

these apples are for grandma.

wash day

Still lost, you wonder
what she could have been: a pea,
a pear, a fist, a princess
strolling in your heels.

The ghost of her hovers
as you clean, a sink
slowly filling with the unlived
and the unbelieved.

We can't let wash day break us
or the children hollering in the streets,
or let their songs remake us,
or be brought down with autumn leaves.

you gotta go there to come back
– Stereophonics

We were out, so it must have been summer;
rocks ready to skull the other, fuelled by love
blind anarchy of a sister and brother. That led to

smashed windows, accusations –
the day we bled the radiators, unhinged
from walls with one another's heads;
the night I slammed your finger
in the fire door. For weeks we watched
the nail blacken and peel away.

I have your features tattooed in me:
your face when you realised I couldn't be held
to the ground anymore, that nature
had granted me unbrotherly strength.
I think that's when you tore
away, and now we've got to go there
to come back, to feel the rocks again,
the burning metal against our skin,
to hear the shatter
of childhood, feel it break and reform.

At the dinner table, you pass me
a glance. We don't shirk memories,
but talk, look over the canvas
of the garden, watch birds prune
and squabble. We know we have to
see each old strike as murmuration:
the fleeting needs
and flocking inclinations.

cat out the bag

A nightmare, slashed
rag of fur, her dead kitten
    dangling
        from her
            half-cut maw.

        Why me?
       I've nothing
     to undo the dead,
          no skill to save
       them. God.

            I lift her
              scrappy sandbag body,
            fill the sink
          with warm water,
           hold her
           under
until the water's red.

          Done.
          I follow
        her trail:

to the sack
where she'd tried
to save her children
but not
understanding
coils
of razor wire,
shattered bottles
she
dragged
them
through
those glistening fields.

abigail

The streets are howling and I'm half drenched.
You push her buggy opposite, lean
against the dog-wet sheet of rain
and she waves from underneath
her forcefield of laminate.

I have walked and nodded
for days in this storm, dodged
roof tiles and traffic cones on my way,
stepped over and through littered streams.
Within this half-hid city all I can take are the drums
of faces, the dreadful innocence, the tormenting beauty.

kintsugi

Futures scarred by dim-lit tracks, break
 like pottery, their wheels   smashed.
 But there's agony in fixing,   understand,
      incubated   hollowed
       coffins   swallowed
       prisms   hatched.
    So we melt   trinkets, gold
   teeth, pretty   hoops and chains,
   fill the fissures   to keep the light
      from leaving   its vessel.

kabuto

The Japanese know how to wrap an apology.
I unfold their kawaii paper – behind four walls
of glass, the rhino beetle marches at me, taps.

Nights pass, we lie awake together. I change
her Petri dish of ochre jelly, call her Kabuto.
She tips the lid, asks *What are we doing here?*

but I've no satisfying answers. At work,
a colleague questions my grape-red lips,
compliments my Japanese work ethic.

I wonder how my beetle counters
her enemies, my absence. I picture her pincers
cutting my colleague's fingers off like cigar heads.

At home, I let her run over my knuckles.
She probes: *How was your day?*
Let's stay together, she says, *forever.*

I say, *I've heard that before.* Gifted,
she's spent the day shaping me
as a jelly figurine. I smile, tighten

the lid of her domicile, relocate
it to the sun-heavy window sill.
It's hot here, she says, wiping her horn

as I leave. *Will you be back soon?*
I lock the door, hear her testing the glass,
repeating: *I need more jelly, more jelly!*

anatman

mango sunrise
almond head
bare feet slow
the monk weaves
rickshaw streets
absorbed
in his holy book

anitya

great orange tip
nut-still
naked core
the butterfly beats
the bustle
unfolds
the pages of its wings

the 200-year-old monk

Like the flower that spawned your stance,
you sit, palms to the sun that never saw you

coming back from the dead. I imagine
a waterfall tumbling above your head,

two centuries of turbulence passing by.
How quiet that tomb must have been,

a fossil, earthed until the present
had enough of your solitude and took it.

Like so much that we cannot untouch,
we've plucked at your petals,

brought them inside to press,
to watch, to wither and know.

songbird

She knows truth
better than me. Scythes
clasping the bark of a branch,
beak ready. Her chest inflates, quicker
than the song that escapes her. Her melody
says sunbathe, vista, mountain highs, but her lyrics
are logger and steel. I imagine her slicing
over castaways, lungs gunning out
the tune she keeps for everyone.
Her wings fold, she lands, soft
as the branch
creaks.

pioneer

i. hyperfine

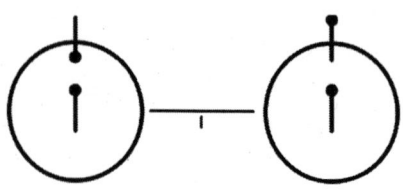

        what are we

atoms spun   thread tied

hello   hallo

helio   halo

        singularity

eye   island

glass   glacier

word   world

        a destination

ii. homo sapien

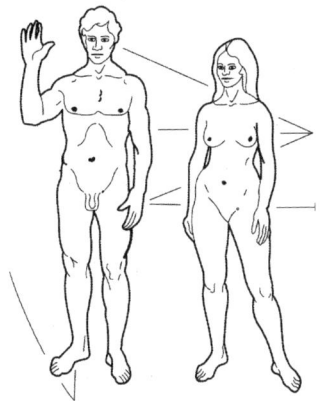

O65 – C18 – H10 – N3 – CA1.4 – P1.1

a mass of life, a basic womb

etched carbon and chromosome

carapace, conch, crustacean

for wild neurons, neutrinos,

bound sacks, a flat space,

a timeline, a memory,

veins, pathogens, tear ducts

hidden, digits raised, exposed

iii. relative

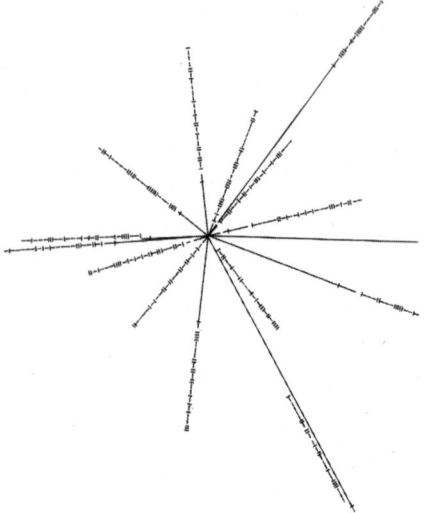

At the next star, turn left. Left. Turn.

You have missed

your exit. Turn

at the next available

You have missed your

You have missed

You have missed

Your destination. Stop.

iv. solar

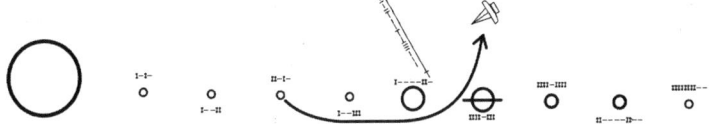

(here we are) in the everafter linear

        (love) and a life marbled spread

gazing outward home (stripped)

        through appetite (yearning) insipid

(ridiculous) loop roof planet

        reclaimed message (drifting) sifted

vacuum (in the darkness) light

        scarcely what remains (repeating)

sending waves (forgettable)

        last and first (transmissions) omissions

here (we are) here come please

        find us we are not (afraid) of reflections

v. craft

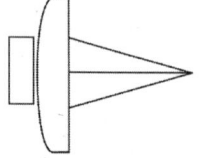

Unscathed, there is space

to recast,

reshape.

A message unset. It is all

that's left of them,

their radiation,

their metal skeleton,

their afterimage burned

on the retina

of light.

It makes nothing

more than itself,

an imperfect trajectory,

turning outwards.

Blow out all the candles.

Under no circumstances should you sing.

They may appear human.

Don't panic. Stay vigilant.

Your morale is vital to international security.

If consumed,

if you hear their

caterwaul,

the alligator get-out clause

Pre-history, an evil eye, sinister-sleek
mississippiensis, walking Appalachian,
taut, primed to roll, a grizzled submarine.

The alligator owns the pool, the 18 holes,
the bayou, parking lot, riverside. Beware
your trespass: ancient, hungry, vacant,

the alligator does not care about your kids,
your direct debits, cholesterol, insurance wavers.
The alligator does not know forgiveness,

is inhumanly patient. Long and quiet, you cease
in its alien eyes. When it moves, don't resist –
the alligator has spent millennia perfecting its bite.

the counting house

That morning we were late: car grunting
white breaths in the winter air. We straightened
ties, brushed our hair. Windows up, we meandered
through the tired city sun. You recited his eulogy
from the back seat; I counted those we'd buried.

Outside, we didn't realise the silence
was his wake, that each glance was held by grief.
We huddled in the shadows of the cemetery.
The hearse pulled in, we stepped aside, the coffin
too short, too wide for the man we remembered.

The bearers struggled to lift the dead
weight on their shoulders. Birds stirred
in the wind. We did what we had to: buried
our hands deep in our pockets, crossed
the threshold and followed them inside.

the good thief

I imagine the CT scans: your withered lungs
like old party balloons, the growing shadows.
Every part of you has been stripped thinner;
even your voice is a contradiction
to my memory of crowds gathering
to hear you sing.

I imagine the weakest nights: bile and phlegm,
another fist of hair gone, and you
begging the dark room to let you be
with her again. Your body and brain
are barely yours but you chirp at the morning
telephone calls to check you're still with us.

I imagine the bones break: too little strength
to hold them together, despite the help, despite
the radiotherapy. Chair-bound now, you still
wave, smile to strangers, shuffle
and struggle for tea, tell your daughters
they are angels, god bless them.

I imagine the line isn't clear: it's far
from me to you. Remember
kiting on the cul-de-sac, the snap of pea pods,
the time your knees were a horse
and we galloped after Robin Hood, the good
thief who gave everything he had.

howls

Out from the tin wall town, the road cools
from hot tyres, horns and shearing
sun. The day's retreated so you don't see
the thick puddle at your feet, but hear
her howl, her growl, her futile panic.

Does she hope to force life
back inside him, or curse the steel
which tore her pup away in two?
Now your eyes adjust, you see
his collarless neck, his newborn head
removed from his body, lids wide,
transfixed at what came for him. Paralysed,

you replay the moment and see yourself
in the throes of his brevity. His mother
wakes the neighbourhood
but it's common here,
where traffic runs like life:
too urgent to stop for anything.
There's no way to fix the unfixable,
so you step away.

october 29th

Frankenstein is knocking
but I've nothing in.
I hunt the corpse
of home for shrapnel,
hope the door stays yolkless.
A dad looms behind his creation, growls
That'd better be at least a quid, so I upgrade
my sacrifice, afraid: the monsters
know where I live.

This dark October screams.
Dogs howl, coiling in their homes,
allow the cats to rule another night.
I pass the all-hours burger joint, where
Alice and the White Rabbit share a shake;
Dracula uncloaks, sinks his fang into a harlot
of bread and pulverised beef; the undead rise
for a shift behind shrieking tills and scalding fries.

Some folks barely make the effort: a mummy's mask
with leopardskin leggings, dad wielding a butter knife,
neck faux-sliced with devil-red lippy. *They're premature,*
I mutter, lugging bags of candy home, and wonder
what they're guising for.

the races

Blood-black and yellow fingertips, like the finches
you bought us after your biggest win, waving
racing slips, a fold of fifties, a whiskeyed grin.
We took the birds home in cages, tattered songs
fresh from the gates until they flew for freedom
and fell, necks broken on the windows.

And you laughed when we cupped our ears
along the hare hills; your misplaced shot
sent the horses and keen boys bolting, bright
eyes and legs burning, the sun swallowed
on your knife edge. You drove us to the races then
to see the fat-fingered, gold-plated men, to learn
the draw and lull of a misspent Sunday
with a chip butty, Bass shandy, a quick dip
in a quiet world, then home again.

I want you to know: we whispered
when you were gone, threw darts
at the furred catch draining on the hook.
Its dark eyes seemed to blink
at us, the nags on the TV, the wild
birds singing through the curtains.

hog

She's apple-mouthed, sides split,
feet bound for the wedding. Skin scored
and salted for crackling, she's javelined,
roasted to perfection, tail to lip.

Her eyes are the hardest to stomach,
too hard to stare into, too familiar.
I think of her snuffling dry leaves,
a litter of oinks following for milk

and push another forkful inside,
glugging a wave of cheap red wine.
At the table we talk about tradition
and ceremony with the pig in our eyes,

the ghost of everybody we've known.
We toast, laugh, try to hold our grief
back to make it through the meal. I can't
help but think of glazed carrots, gravy,

apple sauce, my nan settling hot trays
on the family table; the kids around her
trotters; her silhouette bent
as she raked the garden of dry leaves.

biography of a cow

The cow lies
placid as the grass,
coal and cloud,
milk-heavy, calfless.

Milkers roll nipples
between their fingers,
fill the empty tanks white.
In the abattoir, others beef,
mop-handed. They strip
the cow from the cow.

You are a cow. Check
the health of your hoof, swish
your tail like a metronome
to keep ultimate time.

Rub at the years, forget the fields
of pyres and chemical walkthroughs. Pop
the lid of a lasagne. Pour a tumbler
of semi-skimmed. Calcify. The cow
pushes the grass against its stomach
and calls for the rain.

At the peak is a great old bear, grey and slow.

We can ask about hibernation, but she will reply:

When you sleep do you worry you'll never wake?

ignition

Is it true that we come alive
not once but many times?
– Edwin Morgan

What's born from smithereens?
Heat and flesh, wings that make angels
for an instant. Letters are sent,
news read, and in the drying ink
that instant remains.

The field is the same, but never
the same. The crop, like the earth, rotates,
and the feather which brings the wind
soon lines another nest.

boatswain

The ancient women steer their boats slow
on the drabbles and shallows
of the Mekong. The river pushes
against us, kingfisher to water buffalo.
This is where they come to live
and pray, to see the weeds and oars
rippling in the undertow. Don't fight
the current – our boatswain seems to say –
let the river take you
where it wants to go. Do not swim
in the white waters, do not pan the sand
for gold; you will fail.
She unwraps batons of bamboo
stuffed with rice and salt, sweet
young coconut, smiles
with faded teeth, wet stone eyes,
hands shaking. She stretches a finger
to take us onshore.

She creaks as we climb the banks
to the chicken farm, passing black grills
and red coals. We drink iced lemonade
en route to the fowl huts
where she bolts inside,

fox-like, unfazed
by the chaotic terror mounting
in clucks. Re-emerging, she weighs
the life she has gripped by its leathered feet,
holds a wet knife our way. We shake our heads.
Afterwards, she watches us eat,
scrapes the blood from her fingernails.

let us be mauled by the ocean

I hope we age as beaches do:
whipped cliffs into reefs of sand,
coasts swept into fruit-washed shores.

Let currents bind and tear us in two,
make flotsam of our thighs and hands
and leave us irreversibly sawn.

Dock the orange lifeboats, we'll break through
the white-top waves, dive overboard, stand
bare-foot on urchins and draw

the mollusc from the pearl,
the antenna from the prawn, the land
from snowmelt and estuaries. I want us to pour

dark waters down our sun-lit shirts, unscrew
fine ports, fly crossbone flags to treasure maps,
steer hard into the inevitable storms.

a sleep

You've taken to bed again, your zimmer
by the window. It's early afternoon,
but winter, and soon the day will disappear.
I sit beside you so we can be near.

The clock, like your heart, still ticks.
Dusk brings your breath with it.
The sun tucks itself away. I don't
turn the light on, but stare

at the silhouette of your frame, mechanical,
like a crane hunched over a derelict city.
You groan. Your feet shuffle in your sleep,
dashing through fields near your old home,

towards the stream where we fished,
picked berries, built kites and box cars.
I pull a blanket over you, put on the heat
and the television, watch repeats

of the old movies you loved.
Garland sings about elsewheres
over rainbows, and in the screen's glow
as you hear her words, your lips follow.

up the garden

Our slabbed path fixes again, petunia pink
on sage green through the soil of memory
and I imagine the season's beans climbing,
a plot of lettuce heads. You and me
clasp hands like decades never passed us;
we roll by pansy pots and marigold beds,
past gravestones for long gone cats,
beneath the vine-heavy, white lattice archway.

We cast so many snails
over neighbours' fences.
So many slugs were shrivelled
by our cobalt pellets.
So many of our kites flew
when others fell.

It's hard for us both
not to wither under the past.
Someone's cut the gorse back;
the birds and butterflies have fled.
Your shattered legs won't make it
up the steady steps to the shed,
where our tools have been unheld
too long, and rusted.

So our bones rest in the conservatory,
we see ourselves on plates of glass.
You twist yarns, make me a child again
before the aches end it at last. Somehow,
before we depart, you find enough mercy
to say, *That's nature, however much we hate it.*

balloons over bagan

high enough
to make the world
petite
turn
cattle to ants
sipping sugar cube
lakes
two thousand temples
passed over
like grains of rice
as we race the air

but she is all
I see
another life
I want
to be the wind
that tastes
her tongue
her words
when she speaks

then land
in the cruelty
of croissants and caviar
champagne bubbles
extinguished
by the surface
bitter
sweet
but still
as close as you can get
to flight

aurora photography

We stroll into the night,
look up to the ghost of light
above the yawning city,

seek new stories in the stars,
reform the constellations
to suit our uncertainties.

We try to make a memory
of ourselves, but the flash drains
our faces, deepens the sky

and our photographs reveal a truth
we can't – or aren't willing – to see;
a subtle shift in the dark.

We're good keepers, you and I,
so we take the stars home, prepared
to put them away.

acknowledgements

Massive thanks are due to Duncan Lockerbie and Tapsalteerie for their confidence in my poetry, advice in editing and for their huge efforts in bringing it so beautifully to print.

To the comic artists (Sara Julia Campbell, Caroline Grebbell, Aimee Lockwood, Edward Ross, Mark Toner), thank you so much for your amazing adaptations of my work.

Earthly gratitude goes to the menagerie of people who have helped improve my poems and poetry, including Aileen Ballantyne, Jonathan Bay, Tim Craven, Caroline Hardaker, Alyson Kissner, Dorothy Lawrenson, Matthew Macdonald, Marianne MacRae, Colin McGuire, Alycia Pirmohamed, Lauren Pope, Blythe Robertson, Sarah Stewart, and to Richard Ridgwell for proofreading – I'm really sorry if I've missed anyone, please know that I appreciated your help.

Thank you to my friends and family for their continued support, especially Jo McLaughlin and Pakkun, who allow me to rub their bellies when morale-boosting or inspiration is required.